SCRUB!

A Handy Hand-Washing Guide

ELYSE APRIL

illustrated by

JACQUES LALIBERTÉ

Cover & interior design: Jacques Laliberté, Paulden, Arizona / www.jacqueslaliberte.com

ISBN: 978-1-935826-52-1

Library of Congress Control Number: 2020942282

Kalindi Press
POB 4410
Chino Valley, AZ 86323
www.familyhealthseries.com

Printed in China.

NOTE TO PARENTS & CAREGIVERS

Washing our hands has become as crucial as brushing our teeth. Especially for young children, the eyes, nose, mouth and hands are the primary instruments, since birth, for them to explore their world and collect data. To keep that system healthy, it is important that they learn to wash their hands properly, with warm water and soap and to SCRUB — rubbing the hands vigorously while washing for at least 20 seconds. As their mentors and guardians, it is our responsibility to teach this skill in a loving and non-problematic way that avoids instilling fear of germs and viruses, but emphasizes the necessity to maintain good health practices.

In this simple little book, we have employed the use of an imaginary friend to assist in the instruction of hand-washing. It is not unusual for young children to create such a being. Especially during times of stress, children can imagine a protective guardian as a comfort and security. This is not a replacement for good parenting, but a psychologically sound and normal way for the child to cope — like having their own personal assistant!

We hope you will enjoy reading this book to your child, grandchildren, or any of your young friends who need such a foundation.

Elyse April
Author & Early Childhood Educator

Rub, a dub-dub,

Two hands in a tub.

SOAP

With soap and warm water,
I'm ready to SCRUB!

SOAP
SOAP

Rubbing my hands is part of the plan.

SOAP
SOAP
SOAP
SOAP

I dry with the air, clean towel or a fan.

When my nose drips
I keep my hands clean.
A tissue or hankie
is there on the scene.

Tissue
NEW!

I cover my cough with my arm, not my hand.

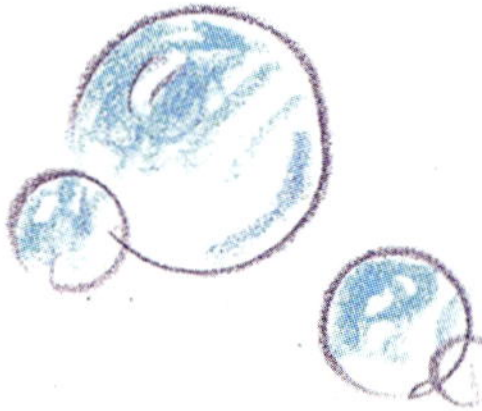

I wash my hands often,
I am taking a stand. . .

. . .to keep myself healthy,
and remember this song.

It takes 20 seconds
To keep myself STRONG!

Rub a dub-dub
Two friends in a tub.

With soap and warm water
I'm ready to . . .

SCRUB!

SCRUB! A Handy Hand-Washing Guide SONG

Rub, a dub-dub, two hands in a tub.

With soap and warm water, I'm ready to SCRUB!

Rubbing my hands is part of the plan.

I dry with the air, a clean towel or a fan.

When my nose drips, I keep those hands clean, a tissue or hankie is there on the scene.

I cover my cough with my arm, not my hand.

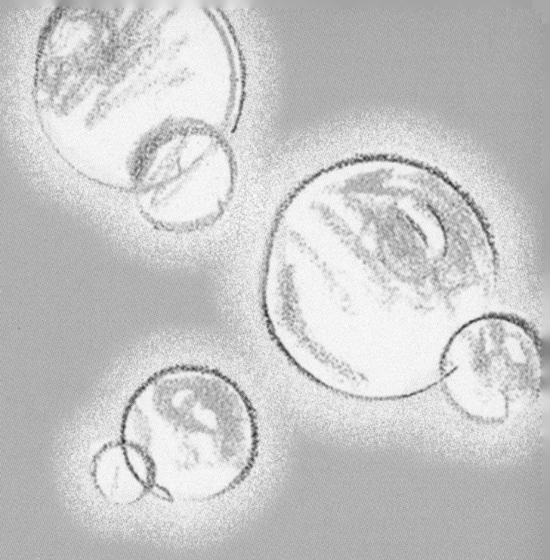

I wash my hands often, I'm taking a stand . . .

. . . to keep myself healthy, and remember this song.

It takes 20 seconds to keep myself STRONG!

Rub a dub-dub, two friends in a tub. With soap and warm water I'm ready to SCRUB!

DEDICATION

This book is dedicated to my friend Karuna who taught me the value of self-care and embodied compassion in action.

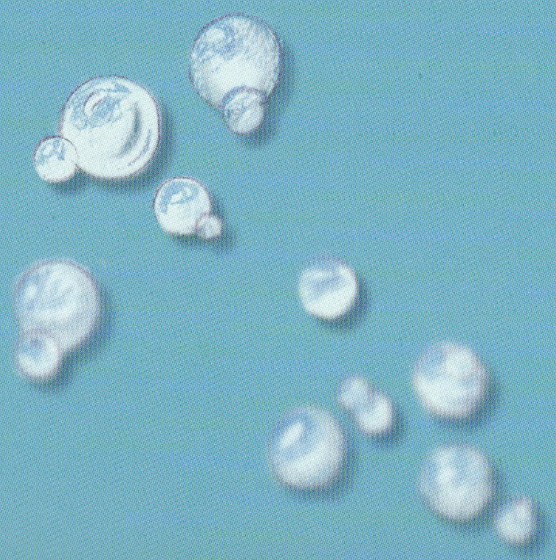

AUTHOR BIO / Elyse April

Elyse April is the Education Director of the Family & World Health Series, the Children's Division of Hohm Press & Kalindi Publishers. She is also founder of "Discover the Hero Within," a program of anti-bullying workshops for teachers, parents and children. Elyse taught elementary and high school students for over twelve years in both public and homeschool settings, was a CPS worker for Child Welfare in Poughkeepsie, NY, as well as a recreation therapist. She has authored many books on children's health and wellness for the Family & World Health series (Hohm/Kalindi Press). She lives in Paulden, Arizona and likes to spend her free time kayaking on nearby lakes.

ILLUSTRATOR BIO / Jacques Laliberté

Artist, illustrator, writer and designer, Jacques has focused on architectural projects in the Northern Arizona area. He has taught college-level drawing and wrote *Raw Draw,* [www.RawDrawtheBook.com] collecting his class lessons about seeing the artistry in our surroundings. Cartooning and whimsical books are on his drawing table these days.

RESOURCES

www.cdc.gov/handwashing/materials.html

wwwitsasnap.org/resources/Handwashing-facts

https://livingmontessorinow.com/handwashing

For Books

www.familyhealthseries.com

www.hohmpress.com

www.kalindipress.com

PARENTING BOOKS

Conscious Parenting, Revised Edition, Lee Lozowick, Hohm Press, 2010

The Conscious Parenting Workbook, Bhadra Mitchell et al, Hohm Press, 2014

Parenting: A Sacred Task, Karuna Fedorschak, Hohm Press, 2003

Heart to Heart, Jeff Goelitz & Elyse April, Hohm Press, 2013

Hold on to Your Kids, Gorden Neufeld, Ballantine Books, 2006

Stand Up! The Courage to Care, Regina Sara Ryan & Elyse April, Hohm Press, 2016

Other Family & World Health Series Titles from Hohm Press / Kalindi Press

AMAZING ANIMALS
That Like to Nurse
by Mary Angelon Young and Ashe Parker
ISBN: 978-1-942493-48-8
Paper, 32 pages, $9.95
Bi-lingual English-Spanish:
978-1-942493-49-5
Paper, 32 pages, $10.95

WE LIKE TO GROW OUR FOOD
by Denise Incao
Illustrations by Valentina Jaskina
ISBN: 978-1-935826-49-1, English;
Paper, 32 pages, $9.95
Bi-lingual English-Spanish:
978-1-935826-48-4
Paper, 32 pages, $10.95

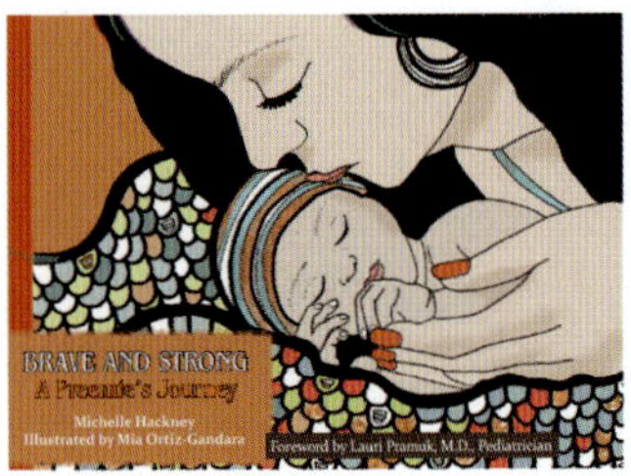

BRAVE AND STRONG
A Preemie's Journey
by Michelle Hackney
Illustrations by Mia Ortiz-Gandara
Foreword by Lauri Pramuk, M.D.
ISBN: 978-1-942493-51-8, English;
Paper, 32 pages, $9.95
Bi-lingual English-Spanish:
978-1-942493-52-5
Paper, 32 pages, $10.95

MAMA'S LECHE
by Michelle Hackney and Mia Ortiz (illustrator)
Bi-lingual English-Spanish:
978-1-942493-24-2
Paper, 32 pages, $10.95

To Order: 800-381-2700 / or visit our websites at
www.familyhealthseries.com / www.hohmpress.com / www.kalindipress.com

Other Family & World Health Series Titles from Hohm Press / Kalindi Press

STAND UP!
The Courage to Care
by Elyse April and Regina Sara Ryan
Illustrations by Maria Oglesby
ISBN: 978-1-942493-17-4
Paper, 32 pages, $9.95

WE LIKE OUR TEETH
by Marcus Allsop
(Text and Illustrations)
ISBN: 978-1-935826-06-4, English;
Paper, 32 pages, $9.95
Bi-lingual English-Spanish:
978-1-935826-09-5
Paper, 32 pages, $10.95

WE LIKE TO NURSE
by Chia Martin
Illustrations by Shukyo Lin Rainey
ISBN: 978-1-934252-45-4, English;
Paper, 32 pages, $9.95
Bi-lingual English-Spanish:
978-1-890772-94-9
Paper, 32 pages, $10.95

READY TO WEAN
by Elyse April
Illustrations by Diane Iverson
ISBN: 978-1-935387-30-5, English;
Paper, 32 pages, $9.95
Bi-lingual English-Spanish:
978-1-935387-60-2
Paper, 32 pages, $10.95

SOAP
SOAP